The Deadly Darts Of The Devil

Dana Rongione

The Deadly Darts of the Devil

Published by

CreateSpace

a DBA of On-Demand Publishing, LLC

All Scripture quotations are taken from the
HOLY BIBLE, King James Version (KJV)

ISBN 978-1448629695

About the Author:

Dana Rongione is a Christian freelance writer in Greenville, SC. Her goal in life is to spread the gospel of Jesus Christ, as well as to encourage other believers. Dana is the author of numerous poems, songs, articles, stories, devotionals, and books.

She has a devotional site at
www.DanaRongione.blogspot.com
and another inspirational site at
www.ChristianSongoftheDay.blogspot.com.

When she's not working, Dana enjoys spending time with her husband, Jason, and her two dogs, Tippy and Mitch. She also enjoys playing the piano, singing, hiking, reading, and of course, writing.

Table of Contents

Introduction

If you have purchased this book, I will assume that you are desiring to gain a deeper understanding of Satan's arsenal in order to better prepare yourself for his attacks. It is true that we, as Christians, are in a spiritual battle. We must fight Satan and his demons every day, but the going gets tricky when we aren't prepared for the oncoming battle. The purpose of this short report is to open your eyes to some of Satan's more subtle attacks. These are the little things that slip in while we are focused on another attack. It is important that we know what we are up against.

For we wrestle not against flesh and blood, but against principalities, against powers, against the rulers of the darkness of this world, against spiritual wickedness in high places. Wherefore take unto you the whole armour of God, that ye may be able to withstand in the evil day, and having done all, to stand. Stand therefore, having your loins girt about with truth, and having on the breastplate of righteousness; And your feet shod with the preparation of the gospel of peace; Above all, taking the shield of faith, wherewith ye shall be able to quench all the fiery darts of

---

the wicked. And take the helmet of salvation, and the sword of the Spirit, which is the word of God. Ephesians 6:12-17

We will leave the topic of the armor of God for another book, but I would like to explore some of the fiery darts. Only by having a knowledge of Satan's arsenal will we have a chance in our daily battles. So, let's get started.

Dart #1: Doubt

Doubt can come in many forms, but we are going to break it down into just three: doubt in ourselves, doubt in others, and doubt in God.

Doubt in ourselves is that nagging feeling that pulls at us constantly. It asks the following questions: Am I really doing God's will? Am I doing everything I should be doing? Am I doing the right thing? Am I capable of doing this? Am I qualified to do this? Are all of my priorities where they should be? While it is a good thing to have an answer to these questions, the questions themselves can cause you to doubt. For example, have you ever prayed about something and gotten peace about it, only to find yourself questioning that peace a few days later?

We are human; therefore, we all make mistakes. But, if we question everything we do, we are creating a constancy for doubt. God is the One who leads our paths. Our lives should follow in His footsteps. If they are not, then, yes, something is wrong, and we should examine our lives. But one of the biggest mistakes we make is convincing ourselves we've taken the wrong road simply because we come upon a road block. God never said this race would be easy. In fact, He says just the opposite. In John 16:33, Jesus said, *These things I have spoken unto you, that in me ye might have peace.* ***In the world ye shall have tribulation:*** *but be of good cheer; I have overcome the world.* Did you catch that? There will be roadblocks. There will be hurdles. There will be pitfalls. Just because we encounter an obstacle does not mean we have made the wrong choices or that we are not able or qualified to finish the race.

It is important in times of self-doubt that we learn to see ourselves as God sees us. To him we are more than conquerors. (Romans 8:37) He sees us through the loving eyes of One who sacrificed His only Son out of love for us. He sees us as forgiven and righteous because when we accepted Christ, we traded in our filthy rags for the righteousness of Christ. We are covered in His blood, and when God looks at us, He doesn't see our failures and our frailty. Instead, He sees our strength and our willingness to serve Him. He doesn't see a child who is *trying* to make it Home. He sees a child who *will* make it Home. That outlook alone ought to make us give up on doubt. We are each special, and while God doesn't need us, He chooses to use us. As long as we stay close to Him, we have no need for doubt, for He will direct our ways. (Proverbs 3:5-6)

Once we have our self-doubt under control, we need to work on our doubt of others. I'm going to use a personal experience as an excellent example of this. I am very involved in my church. I am the Sunday School teacher for the teenage girls, I am the full-time pianist, and my husband and I are the youth leaders. On top of that, we fill in here and there whenever needed. I like being involved. I am thrilled that God is able and willing to use me in so many ways in our local church. However, my many responsibilities don't leave me much time for fellowship unless people come early or stay late. This was brought to my attention recently when a fellow church member stopped me on my way to the piano and told me that I had not spoken to them for the past three services. Not knowing what else to say, I muttered an apology and headed to the piano. After church, my husband, Jason, questioned me about my strange mood. I burst into tears and said, "Everybody thinks I'm a snob because I don't talk to them at church." I went on to explain to him that I wasn't trying to avoid people, but that my many responsibilities often hindered me from just sitting around and chatting. I told him about my confrontation that morning and assured him that if this person felt that way, the rest of the church did too. I had convinced myself that the entire church thought of me as a snob because one person had made a comment to me. I doubted the whole congregation based on one person's criticism.

I don't know if you've ever had a situation like that, but I'm sure we've all had times that we've doubted what someone said or thought. We often have that feeling that people tell us one thing when they feel entirely different. Why do we do that? Why can't we just give people the benefit of the doubt and assume that they mean what they say? Doubt can cause such confusion!

The worst doubt of all comes about when we start doubting God. Now, for all of you who are much holier than I am, you can skip this section. But, for the rest of you, hear me out because this is important. There will come a time (or you may have already faced it) when your faith in God will crumble. It may be one big trial. It could be after a series of little trials. But, there will come a time when you will look up into the sky and cry, "God, I thought you cared about me, but if that's true, you wouldn't have allowed this to happen!" You may find yourself standing by the grave of a loved one and asking the Great Physician why He didn't heal them. You may find yourself buried in debt, constantly wondering why God isn't keeping His promises about supplying all your needs. You may find yourself walking through the valley and questioning if God is really with you after all. Trust me. If you haven't already faced it, it will come. The question is, what will you do when those doubts arise?

The best thing to do is to memorize the many promises of God. Below are some of my favorites:

Let your conversation be without covetousness; and be content with such things as ye have: for he hath said, I will never leave thee, nor forsake thee. - Hebrews 13:5

And we know that all things work together for good to them that love God, to them who are the called according to his purpose. - Romans 8:28

But they that wait upon the LORD shall renew their strength; they shall mount up with wings as eagles; they shall run, and not be weary; and they shall walk, and not faint. - Isaiah 40:31

I will lift up mine eyes unto the hills, from whence cometh my help. My help cometh from the LORD, which made heaven and earth. He will not suffer thy foot to be moved: he that keepeth thee will not slumber. Behold, he that keepeth Israel shall neither slumber nor sleep. The LORD is thy keeper: the LORD is thy shade upon thy right hand. The sun shall not smite thee by day, nor the moon by night. The LORD shall preserve thee from all evil: he shall preserve thy soul. The LORD shall preserve thy going out and thy coming in from this time forth, and even for evermore. Psalm 121

They that sow in tears shall reap in joy. He that goeth forth and weepeth, bearing precious seed, shall doubtless come again with rejoicing, bringing his sheaves with him. - Psalm 126:5-6.

But, it's not enough to just memorize them. You must commit yourself to them. You must claim them. You must tell yourself that no matter what happens, you know God's promises are true. You must know His promises with your heart and not just your head. This is your best defense against doubt. So, the next time you find yourself wondering if God really cares about you, claim one of His promises, and hold onto it with all the strength you have left. He cares, and He will come through for you. Have faith! *That your faith should not stand in the wisdom of men, but in the power of God. I Corinthians 2:5.*

I think probably one of the best examples of doubt in the Bible is the children of Israel. Time after time, God supplied their needs, yet it was never enough. He gave them manna, and they worried about their thirst. He gave them water from the rock, and they doubted He would provide direction. He led them by a cloud and a pillar of fire, yet they

Page 13

complained that God didn't care and that things would have been better if they had stayed in Egypt. When God said they could conquer the land, they looked at the giants and said, "No, there's just no way!"

I'm quick to point my finger at the children of Israel and say, "What are you thinking? God has proven His love and ability over and over again. Why do you still doubt Him?" But, how many times do I do the same thing? I've seen God do great and mighty things. I've seen Him pay the bills when the bank account was empty. I've seen Him heal the sick when the doctor had given up hope. I've seen Him change a life into something no one ever imagined it could be. I've seen Him work miracles. So, why, when faced with hard times, do I get spiritual amnesia? Why don't I think back on all the times God has seen me through and realize that He will see me through again? Why? Doubt!

Doubt is a deadly dart, and it slips in when you least expect it. Beware!

Dart #2 – Disappointment

Everyone, at one time or another, has faced the bitter sting of disappointment. The job you were perfect for was given to someone else. The raise you were anticipating fell through. You husband said he wouldn't miss dinner again, but the meatloaf is cold, and he's still not home. Disappointment! It's hit all of us.

In fact, if you flip through the pages of your Bible, you'll find story after story about disappointment. Yes, there are many wonderful things in the Bible. There are stories of miracles and of happy endings. But, there are also tales of people hurting —those who have faced disappointment.

Allow me to draw your attention to some well-known women of the Bible. Sarai, Rachel, Hannah, and Elizabeth all faced the shame and heart-breaking disappointment of being barren. In today's society, it's acceptable for a woman to not have a child, whether it be because of physical problems or by choice. But, back in the Bible times, having children was the mark of a woman. For a woman not to have a child was not only a shame to her, but to her husband, as well. Can you imagine the ridicule these women must have faced? Here they are, trying to serve the Lord and do what's right, and what is their reward? Laughter, pointing, whispers of mockery. If only they had known what we know now.

What about Job and Joseph? When I read their stories, I am so convicted. I'm afraid if I had to face what they faced, my faith would not be as strong. Yet, you know that, even with their strong faith, they must have grown disappointed at times. Can't you see Joseph sitting in the jail cell thinking, *I was fleeing from evil. I was trying to keep something bad from happening. I was doing what was right. Why am I being punished?* I would be.

And Job, in his disappointment said, *My soul is weary of my life; I will leave my complaint upon myself; I will speak in the bitterness of my soul. I will say unto God, Do not condemn me; shew me wherefore thou contendest with me. Is it good unto thee that thou shouldest oppress, that thou shouldest despise the work of thine hands, and shine upon the counsel of the wicked? (Job 10:1-3)*

Yes, even in the midst of a strong faith, disappointment can arise.

The disciples are another group that faced true disappointment. Though they traveled with Jesus for over three years, they just didn't grasp all that He had been trying to teach them. Jesus had tried to explain to them that He was not here to set up an earthly kingdom. He was here to minister and to provide a sacrifice so that others could live in eternity with Him. But, as great a teacher as Jesus was, the disciples never got it.

See their disappointment as they sit in a dark room the day after the crucifixion. See their confusion as they try to figure out what to do next. All of their dreams, all of their hopes, all of their expectations were now sealed in the tomb of their Master. Yes, death has quite a sting, but so does disappointment.

Mary and Martha felt that sting as well. Dear friends of Jesus, they felt sure that He would heal their brother, Lazarus. After all, Jesus had healed many people. But, when their pleas were made, Jesus tarried. Only after Lazarus had died did Jesus show up on the scene. Do you hear the disappointment in Martha's voice, *Lord, if thou hadst been here, my brother had not died*? Mary's cry echoes that of Martha. Why had Jesus not come? Why had He allowed Lazarus to die? We know the answer to those questions because we have the entire story. Mary and Martha didn't.

But, probably the most disappointed character in the Bible was John the Baptist. This man spent his entire life paving the way for Christ. He taught. He baptized. He pointed souls to the Lamb of God. From the time he was in the womb, he couldn't wait to tell others about the Savior. But, when times became tough, John began to doubt. And then that doubt led to a growing disappointment. Listen to the words he spoke from his jail cell. *Now when John had heard in the prison the works of Christ, he sent two of his disciples, and said unto him, Art thou he that should come, or do we look for another?* John was beginning to wonder if his whole life had been in vain.

If you read on in the story, you'll notice that Jesus was not offended by John's question. You see, many people will tell you that it is a sin to be disappointed. That's not so. The sin lies in how you handle that disappointment. For example, if you allow that disappointment to cause you to grow bitter, that is a sin. Instead, allow disappointment to cause you to grow better.

Bitterness has never helped anyone. I once read a saying that went something like this, "Bitterness is like drinking a poison and then waiting for the other person to die." That's so true. Bitterness doesn't hurt others. It hurts you! When you feel disappointment leading you to ask, "Why, Lord?," turn that question into "What now, Lord?"

We know from reading the Bible that God had a plan for all of those who faced disappointment. The barren women later had children who played vital roles in the history of Israel. Job and Joseph went on to accomplish great things and to be greatly rewarded for their suffering. The disciples finally understood what Christ had been trying to tell them, and they each spent the rest of their lives spreading the news far and wide. Mary and Martha witnessed a miracle when Jesus resurrected their brother, Lazarus. And even though John the

Baptist did die in prison, can you imagine the homecoming he received when he was carried to Heaven and stood before The King of Kings? Everything worked out according to God's plan.

The hard thing we face is that we can't see the entire story of our own lives. We don't know where the disappointment will lead or how God will use it in our lives. However, we do know that God has our best interest at heart. We know He has a plan, and sometimes that plan involves disappointment. Does that make it any easier to face? In a lot of ways, no, it doesn't. But, there is a peace in knowing that God is in control of our lives, both the good and the bad. It's good to know that when we face disappointment, we can go to Him, and He will help bear our burdens. I like the words to the old hymn, "Tell It to Jesus."

Are you weary, are you heavy hearted?
Tell it to Jesus, tell it to Jesus.
Are you grieving over joys departed?
Tell it to Jesus alone.

Do the tears flow down your cheeks unbidden?
Tell it to Jesus, tell it to Jesus.

Have you sins that to men's eyes are hidden?
Tell it to Jesus alone.

Do you fear the gathering clouds of sorrow?
Tell it to Jesus, tell it to Jesus.
Are you anxious what shall be tomorrow?
Tell it to Jesus alone.

Are you troubled at the thought of dying?
Tell it to Jesus, tell it to Jesus.
For Christ's coming kingdom are you sighing?
Tell it to Jesus alone.

Tell it to Jesus, tell it to Jesus,
He is a Friend that's well-known.
You've no other such a friend or brother,
Tell it to Jesus alone.

"Disappointment to a noble soul is what cold water is to burning metal; it strengthens, tempers, intensifies, but never destroys it." - Eliza Tabor

Dart #3 – Discouragement

Old Fable:

In the devil's marketplace were found many tools. Tools such as deceit, lying, jealously, pride, hatred, envy, etc. were all up for sale at discount prices. However, in the corner of the room, there was another tool, separated from the rest. It was well-protected and encased in glass as a means of protection from the dust. Unlike the other tools, its price was high. This tool was discouragement. When asked why such a small tool was so highly priced, the devil answered, "It is the most terrific of them all. It can pry open a heart no matter how shielded. It gets inside a heart when I cannot. Adultery, idolatry, hatred, etc. have my labels placed upon them, and so people will know it's coming from me. But not so with discouragement. You see how badly worn it is? Because I use it on almost everyone, and few people know it belongs to me."

* *

Discouragement is defined as "a feeling of despair in the face of obstacles; a state of distress and loss of sense of enthusiasm, drive, or courage." Has anyone ever felt like that?

Discouragement has always been real, but I think recently, we've seen it in new levels. With the current economic crisis, there are hundreds of thousands of discouraged people looking for jobs and ways to feed their families. Homes are being foreclosed. Companies are shutting down. Extremely qualified business men and women are standing in line to fill out applications at the local fast food chains. Yes, discouragement is all around us.

Unfortunately, I know this topic very well, for discouragement has hit my home as well. At the beginning of the year, my husband, Jason, was laid off. There was no warning. He was called into a meeting where his boss explained that many of their projected earnings had been pulled away from them, so they would have to cut back on their employees. With that, he was unemployed. From one day to the next, we went from financial security to complete uncertainty.

At first, we weren't overly concerned. After all, we knew that God would take care of us like He always had. Plus, Jason is a good worker. We knew it wouldn't be long before the Lord led him to the "perfect job."

But now, nearly four months have passed, and Jason is still out of work. I'll admit that I've cried more than my fair share of tears. There have been times that I've cried out to God only to find that I didn't have the words to express what I was feeling or what I was in need of. At times, I've been angry. Most of the time, I've been confused. *God, what are You doing? What are You trying to show us? What do we do now?*

But, more than anything, I've felt the cold hand of discouragement gripping me so hard that I could barely breathe. I've faced the feeling that everything I've worked for has been in vain. I've been to the point where I've looked at what others had and cried, "It's just not fair!" (We'll talk more about this in another chapter.)

Discouragement can suck the joy right out of life. It can warp our focus to where all we can see is the negative all around us. Worst of all, discouragement leads to the desire to give up on everything, including God. Discouragement argues, "Look, you've tried. You've done what's right. You've lived by God's standard. Now, what has it gotten you?" And sadly, we listen, and that is where our trouble begins.

I mentioned earlier about the disappointment the disciples must have faced after the death of Christ. But, the really dangerous thing about the darts of the devil is that they never come alone. On the heels of the great disappointment, Peter makes this proclamation, "I go a fishing." I don't think Peter intended for this to be a pleasure trip. I don't think he just wanted to get out and get some fresh air. I think Peter was going back to his old job, his old way of life. In essence, I think Peter was saying, "Well, it was good while it lasted, but now Jesus is gone, and I need to get back to work. I gave it a try, but it just didn't work out, so I quit." Do you his discouragement?

As if that weren't bad enough, the other disciples decided to join him. Isn't it amazing how easy it is to get others to follow us down the wrong path? If only it were that easy to lead others down the right path. But, discouragement is very persuasive and quite contagious!

To illustrate just how much discouragement can change our outlook, I want to share with you two quotes that I found. Read them carefully.

Quote #1:

> *It is difficult to make a man miserable*
> *while he feels he is worthy of himself and*
> *claims kindred to the great God who made him.*

Quote #2:

> *I am now the most miserable man living.*
> *If what I feel were equally distributed*
> *to the human family, there would not be one*
> *cheerful face on earth. Whether I shall be*
> *better I cannot tell. I actually forebode I shall not.*

To remain as I am is impossible. I must die

or be better.

Isn't it amazing that two people could have such different views of life? You want to know what's even more amazing? The above quotations were both spoken by the same person in different times of his life. Yes, even Abraham Lincoln knew what it was like to face discouragement.

While there is no true "cure" for discouragement, there are some things we can do to keep it at bay.

First of all, we need rest. Yes, I'm speaking of physical rest. It is an accepted fact that when our bodies are tired, we are more susceptible to mood changes and stress. However, as important as that is, it is also important to get our spiritual rest. Psalm 37:7 says, *Rest in the Lord, and wait patiently for him.* To rest in the Lord means to lean on Him, to cast our cares upon Him. The word "rest" implies peace and comfort. These can be found by going to God and sharing with Him the source of our discouragement. Then, lean on His strength to see us through.

Second, we need to reflect. This takes some practice, but it's worth it. Reflecting means taking all of our negative thoughts and turning them into positive ones. For example, my husband lost his job and hasn't worked in four months. That's a very negative thought, and dwelling on it leads to discouragement. Reflection teaches me to turn that thought around and look for the good in it. Yes, my husband lost his job, but we've been able to spend a lot of time together lately. Family time is important to us, and because of our current situation, we get a lot of it. Do you see the shift in our outlook? Bad circumstance? Yes, but what good came from it? Sometimes, we have to look really hard, and when all else fails, reflect on Romans 8:28 that reminds us if good hasn't come out of it yet, it will!

Third, we need to resist the devil who will be shouting at us constantly. No, it's not an audible voice, but sometimes it feels like he's sitting right on our shoulders, filling our ears with complaints and negative thoughts. It's easy to listen to him without even realizing we're doing it. That's why we need to become more aware of his presence. If the thoughts we're having are negative and leading to discouragement, they're not of God. II Corinthians 10:5 speaks of *bringing into captivity every thought to the obedience of Christ.* When we resist the devil, that's the first step in getting our thoughts straight. Once he's no longer shouting in our ears, it's easier to bring those thoughts to where they need to be.

Dart #4 – Disillusionment

Here's a topic we don't see dealt with very often these days, but it's still a major problem. Disillusion is very similar to doubt, but with disillusionment, the truth is not only questioned, it is replaced.

Disillusion literally means "to free from illusion; to cause to lose naive faith and trust." Some popular synonyms include "enlighten, set straight, undeceive." When you read that, disillusionment sounds like a good thing, but the devil has a way of making good things bad. He seeks to "enlighten" us with the things that we're missing out on by serving God. He connives to "set us straight" on the path that we feel would bring us the most money or the most happiness. His greatest desire is to "cause us to lose faith and trust" in Christ, our Lord and Savior. Yes, disillusionment can be a good thing, but a good thing in the hands of an enemy is dangerous!

For a good example of how the devil uses disillusionment, check out a few commercials on television or advertisements in the newspaper. People are promising the world!

Join this health club, and you're guaranteed to lose 50 lbs. in the first month.

I made $10,000 my first day on the job, and you can too!

Anyone can write a book. . .even if they failed high school English.

Come in today for the greatest sale ever!

Sound familiar? Now, I'm not saying that there aren't legitimate commercials and advertisements out there. I'm just saying that you have to weed through the "junk" in order to find them. Sadly, many people today are in the business of deceiving others. Many people will do whatever it takes to make a few bucks, even if it means promising something that they can never deliver.

Satan's attacks with disillusionment are first recorded with the fall of Adam and Eve. When Satan tempted Eve with the fruit from the tree, he first questioned the Word of God. *Yea, hath God said, Ye shall not eat of every tree of the garden?*

Ye shall not surely die: for God doth know that in the day ye eat thereof, then your eyes shall be opened, and ye shall be as gods, knowing good and evil.

In the blink of an eye, he implements three of his most powerful weapons: doubt, deceit, and disillusionment. He leads Eve to believe that she's been lied to or tricked. He convinces her that there is more to life than just taking care of the garden. He paints a picture that presented Eve as a god, equal to THE GOD.

Unfortunately, Satan's attacks have not ended there. While doing the research for this book, I came across a couple of web sites that caught me off-guard. They were sites designed and intended for ex-Christians.

My first thought was *How do you become an ex-Christian?* I'll admit, I was intrigued, so I went in and looked around. Wow! You talk about some people who are disillusioned! The site was set up to where members could come in and explain why they "left the faith." Here were some of the top reasons:

1.) I just never fit in at the church. The people weren't friendly.

2.) I didn't feel the desire to serve the Lord.

3.) I found out that God really wasn't loving and caring at all.

4.) Beloved stories of the Bible fall apart under critical scrutiny.

5.) I guess I just don't have enough faith.

As I read through the accounts on these sites, my heart broke. Were these people really saved to begin with, and if so, what happened to cause such great doubt? There were some posts that were written by people who claimed to be Christians for over 40 years. Their reason for "leaving the faith" was that it just didn't make sense anymore, and that it was time to face reality. How sad!

I don't know if these people were truly saved or not. Only God can know that. But, if they were, Satan has definitely used something or someone to cause them to deny their faith.

They have been disillusioned from the truth. They have been made to believe a lie.

There are many times in our lives when Satan can slip in and start pushing our buttons. Just like Eve, he brings his best weapons. "Does God even care about you?" he whispers. During those times of a lost job, an unsuccessful pregnancy, the loss of a loved one, a fading ministry, it's easy to heed those seeds of doubt that the devil plants. Before long, that doubt can turn to disillusionment, and in the end, a complete denial of faith in God.

The key to battling disillusionment can be found in Psalm 73. In verses 1-16, you'll witness a first-class pity party (very similar to the ones we throw from time to time). Listen to the psalmist's complaints:

1 Truly God is good to Israel, even to such as are of a clean heart.

2 But as for me, my feet were almost gone; my steps had well nigh slipped.

3 For I was envious at the foolish, when I saw the prosperity of the wicked.

4 For there are no bands in their death: but their strength is firm.

5 They are not in trouble as other men; neither are they plagued like other men.

6 Therefore pride compasseth them about as a chain; violence covereth them as a garment.

7 Their eyes stand out with fatness: they have more than heart could wish.

8 They are corrupt, and speak wickedly concerning oppression: they speak loftily.

9 They set their mouth against the heavens, and their tongue walketh through the earth.

10 Therefore his people return hither: and waters of a full cup are wrung out to them.

11 And they say, How doth God know? and is there knowledge in the most High?

12 Behold, these are the ungodly, who prosper in the world; they increase in riches.

13 Verily I have cleansed my heart in vain, and washed my hands in innocency.

14 For all the day long have I been plagued, and chastened every morning.

15 If I say, I will speak thus; behold, I should offend against the generation of thy children.

16 When I thought to know this, it was too painful for me;

Ouch! Do you hear the despair? Do you see the uncertainty? I'll admit, I've had times when this was my song as well. Why do the wicked prosper? Why are the wicked swimming in pools of money when I can't even afford to pay my bills? I'm trying so hard to serve You. I've gone where You directed. I've done what You commanded. Why am I being punished?

Doesn't it sometimes feel like the whole world is out to get you? That's exactly what Satan wants. He wants us to be so completely overwhelmed that we'll turn anywhere for answers. . .even if those answers are the wrong ones. So, how do we stop that from happening? Look at verse 17 in the same chapter of Psalms.

17 Until I went into the sanctuary of God; then understood I their end.

Wow! That's good. The presence of God can make a big difference. Please understand, God is always present. He is always with us, and He will always be with us. But, we are not always aware of His presence. We need to be. Think about it for a minute. If God, in human form, were sitting here with me right now, do you think I'd be worried about what's going on with the wicked? In the presence of the Almighty Judge, do you think I would be wringing my hands and wondering why life wasn't fair? Chances are, probably not. So, why do we do it now?

We are in the presence of The Mighty God. Why should we be worried about anything? Better yet, why should we question His Word when He's proven Himself to us time and time again?

Being in God's presence is important, but it's also important to be around God's people. We shouldn't meet together for church services because we're required to. We should gather together because we want to and we need to! We need to hear the Gospel presented in word and song. We need to fellowship with other believers. What a joy it is to be able to share our burdens with others, knowing that their prayers are with us. That's what church is all about.

So, if you're facing questions and doubts today, don't fear. Go to the sanctuary! Study the Word and find the answers you've been seeking. Take your burdens, your uncertainties, and your worries. Give them to God and receive His peace in exchange.

Dart #5 – Depression

Everyone feels "down" from time to time. That's just part of life. But, there are times when we sink so far in despair that life becomes unbearable. This is a good sign that we are falling into a depression.

There are different levels of depression. Some people use the word "depressed" to describe feelings of discouragement, frustration, or sadness. This is known as "situational depression," and it is usually brought on by circumstances. While this type of depression is a normal part of life, repetition of these dark times can lead to the mental illness known as "clinical depression."

During these times, people are completely overwhelmed by life and its circumstances. Even the tasks and hobbies that they once enjoyed become troublesome and un-relaxing. Some sufferers are weighed down by sadness, while others simply feel lifeless and empty. Some symptoms of depression include the following:

- Sleeplessness or sleeping too much

- Inability to concentrate

- Feelings of hopelessness

- Overeating or not eating enough

- Constantly irritated or frustrated

- Loss of energy; fatigue

- Feelings of guilt

- Excessive crying

- Overwhelming despair

- Thoughts of suicide

While several of these symptoms can be associated with other illnesses, many suicides are the result of depression. People feel trapped, unable to find joy in life, unable to experience pleasure. They look for solutions in medication and various therapy sessions, but in the end, it seems that nothing will stop their pain. While sitting alone in that dark abyss, they see death as their only option.

Whether or not depression is a true illness or simply a state of mind, I do not know. Nor do I wish to argue the subject. What I do know is that "situational depression" becomes "clinical depression" because it is not dealt with in the first place. Because gloomy times are a part of life, we simply sweep them under the rug and try to carry on. This won't work. As much as we don't want to, we must deal with these emotions and get them straightened out before they escalate into bigger problems.

Depression, as with the other darts, can be seen all throughout the Bible. In fact, I believe it all started with Adam and Eve. Now, the Bible doesn't say anything here about depression. I'm just reading between the lines a little. Adam and Eve sinned, and because of that sin, they were cursed and thrown out of the garden. Don't you think they felt a little depressed? Don't you think they suffered feelings of guilt or worthlessness? Don't you think they had some trouble sleeping for a while? Don't you think they were engulfed with sadness at having to leave their perfect home? Yes, I think there was probably some depression going on.

Another good example follows on the heels of one of my favorite Bible stories. I Kings 18 tells the story. Elijah challenged the prophets of Baal to a little contest.

And Elijah said unto the prophets of Baal, Choose you one bullock for yourselves, and dress it first; for ye are many; and call on the name of your gods, but put no fire under. (vs. 25)

So, the prophets of Baal accepted the challenge. They built their altar and laid the bull upon it. Then, the fun began. They called to their god to send fire down. All morning long they called and called, but nothing happened. You can imagine the smirk on Elijah's face when he said,

Cry aloud: for he is a god; either he is talking, or he is pursuing, or he is in a journey, or peradventure he sleepeth, and must be awakened. (vs. 27)

And so, they cried louder and began cutting themselves with knives and lancets and jumping up and down on the altar. Still, there was no answer to their prayers. (For those of you who are wondering, there was no answer because the "god" they were praying to didn't exist.)

Finally, Elijah told them to stop and gather around his altar. He rebuilt the altar, laid the bullock on top, and then made a strange request. He ordered barrel after barrel of water to be poured over the altar. The water drenched the altar, soaking into the wood and rock and leaving a pool around the base of the altar itself. He offered a prayer to God, asking Him to send down fire to prove to these people once and for all who is the true God. God responded by sending down a fire intense enough to burn the wood, the rocks, the dirt, and to soak up all the water. Now, that's some fire! The people were convinced and the prophets of Baal were destroyed. All in all, it seemed like a good day. Then, problems arose.

And Ahab told Jezebel all that Elijah had done, and withal how he had slain all the prophets with the sword. Then Jezebel sent a messenger unto Elijah, saying, So, let the gods do to me, and more also, if I make not thy life as the life of one of them by to morrow about this time. (I Kings 19:1-2)

How did Elijah respond? With another prayer? Another great display of the Lord's power? Nope, he ran!

And when he saw that, he arose, and went for his life, and came to Beer-sheba, which belongeth to Judah, and left his servant there. But he himself went a day's journey into the wilderness, and came and sat down under a juniper tree: and he requested for himself that he might die; and said, It is enough; now, O LORD, take away my life; for I am not better than my fathers. (I Kings 19:3-4)

Do you see the hopelessness? Do you hear the despair as he pleads with God to let him die? How, after such a great victory, could he now be ready to give up his life and his ministry? Easy. He took his eyes off of God and put them on himself and his circumstances. And that, my friend, is the first step into depression.

When hard times come in life, it is more important than ever to keep our focus on God. He is our source of light. He is guiding us along life's road. He is our Comforter and best Friend. So, is it any wonder that when we take our eyes off Him we feel like we're sinking in darkness, lost and all alone? We need to keep our focus. Only then can we see beyond our troubles. Here are a few Scriptures that may help:

- *And the Lord, he it is that doth go before thee; he will be with thee; he will not fail thee, neither forsake thee: fear not, neither be dismayed. (Deuteronomy 31:8)*

- *Arise, shine; for thy light is come, and the glory of the LORD is risen upon thee. (Isaiah 60:1)*

- *These things I have spoken unto you, that in me ye might have peace. In the world ye shall have tribulation: but be of good cheer; I have overcome the world. (John 16:33)*

- *Beloved, think it not strange concerning the fiery trial which is to try you, as though some strange thing happened unto you: But rejoice, inasmuch as ye are partakers of Christ's sufferings; that, when his glory shall be revealed, ye may be glad also with exceeding joy. (I Peter 4:12-13)*

- *Let not your heart be troubled: ye believe in God, believe also in me. In my Father's house are many mansions: if it were not so, I would have told you. I go to prepare a place for you. And if I go and prepare a place for you, I will come again, and receive you unto myself; that where I am, there ye may be also. (John 14:1-3)*

- *And we know that all things work together for good to them that love God, to them who are the called according to his purpose. (Romans 8:28)*

- *Humble yourselves therefore under the mighty hand of God, that he may exalt you in due time: Casting all your care upon him; for he careth for you. (I Peter 5:6-7)*

- *O Lord, thou hast searched me, and known me. Thou knowest my downsitting and mine uprising, thou understandest my thought afar off. Thou compassest my path and my lying down, and art acquainted with all my ways. For there is not a word in my tongue, but, lo, O LORD, thou knowest it altogether. Thou hast beset me behind and before, and laid thine hand upon me. Such knowledge is too wonderful for me; it is high, I cannot attain unto it. Whither shall I go from thy spirit? or whither shall I flee from thy presence? If I ascend up into heaven, thou art there: if I make my bed in hell, behold, thou art there. If I take the wings of the morning, and dwell in the uttermost parts of the sea; Even there shall thy hand lead me, and thy right hand shall hold me. If I say, Surely the darkness shall cover me; even the night* shall be light about me. Yea, the darkness hideth not from thee; but the night shineth as the day: the darkness and the light are both alike to thee. For thou hast possessed my reins: thou hast covered me in my mother's womb. I will praise thee; for I am fearfully and wonderfully made: marvellous are thy works; and that my soul knoweth right well. My substance was not hid from thee, when I was made in secret, and curiously wrought in the lowest parts of the earth. Thine eyes did see my substance, yet being unperfect; and in thy book all my members were written, which in continuance were fashioned, when as yet there was none of them. How precious also are thy thoughts unto me, O God! how great is the sum of them! If I should count them, they are more in number than the sand: when I awake, I am still with thee. Surely thou wilt slay the wicked, O God: depart from me therefore, ye bloody men. For they speak against thee wickedly, and thine enemies take thy name in vain. Do not I hate them, O LORD, that hate thee? and am not I grieved with those that rise up against thee? I hate them with perfect hatred: I count them mine enemies. Search me, O God, and know my *heart: try me, and know my thoughts: And see if there be any wicked way in me, and lead me in the way everlasting. (Psalm 139)*

Dart #6 – Defeat

Have you ever been prevailed over or deprived of something you were expecting? Have you ever lost a battle or a contest? If so, then you know the acrid taste of defeat. If we're not careful, defeat can easily lead us into one of the other deadly darts, like discouragement, doubt, and depression.

To illustrate this point, I want to use another personal experience. It was late July a couple of years ago. The temperature was somewhere around 100°. My husband and I discovered that we had a huge leak somewhere around the outside pipe to which the water hose was attached.

We started at the task early, hoping to get most of the work done before the temperature became sweltering. No such luck! The sun was beating down on us. Sweat poured from us as we dug deeper and deeper into the earth, trying to reach the pipe so that we could repair it.

Finally, we found the pipe and discovered that it had not one, but two holes in it, from which water was spewing. Knowing the pipe would have to be replaced, we unscrewed it from the other pipe that it was attached to and stuffed flower putty down inside the hole to keep the water from gushing out until we could get back with the new pipe. (Now, I know some of you are scratching your head and saying, "Flower putty?" It's what I could find at the time. Okay?)

Fortunately, the store is not far from our house, so we took the pipe, drove to the store, bought a new one, and came back home. We were gratified to see that the flower putty had held and that the hole was not full of water. (See, my idea wasn't so dumb after all!)

We worked for several more minutes, removing the putty and threading in the new pipe. I thought we were finished, but Jason insisted that the pipe was crooked and needed to be straightened. So, he pushed the pipe. . .and it broke!

Now we had a broken pipe, part of which was stuck inside the other pipe which was now gushing water and filling up the hole. Jason looked at me in horror, and I did the only thing I could think to do at the time. I laughed!

Those of you who know me well know this is not my typical reaction. Usually when faced with such utter defeat, I cry. All I can say is that the Lord must have given me grace and strength because all I could do was laugh. Within minutes, Jason was laughing with me. Meanwhile, the hole was overflowing with water, and the broken pipe was lying on the ground.

We hopped back in the truck, went back to the store, bought another pipe and a screw extraction kit to get the other end of the pipe unstuck, and hurried home to try again. First, we had to get the water out of the hole and stop the leak (yes, more flower putty). Then, thankfully, we were able to remove the piece of the old pipe and replace it with the new one. We left it crooked, filled in the hole, and went inside to take a much-needed shower.

Defeat, in and of itself, is not a problem. After all, both teams can't win the ballgame, can they? It is how we handle the defeat that becomes the problem. The story I just told you is an example of a time when I handled defeat in the right way. I laughed. I didn't let it discourage me. I went on and tried again. Unfortunately, I don't always handle it that way, and that is when defeat turns deadly.

* *

It is inevitable that some defeat will enter even the most victorious life. The human spirit is never finished when it is defeated. . .it is finished when it surrenders. - Ben Stein

* *

Need another example? How about the children of Israel? I know it seems like I pick on them a lot, and I promise that is not my intention. It's simply that their deeds fit so well with what I'm discussing. If anyone walked around in defeat, it was the children of Israel. Take a look at their trek through the wilderness.

Not only were they constantly complaining, but look at how many times they simply gave up. Examine their cries of "We want to go back to Egypt." Their fatigue and unhappiness had defeated them. They had convinced themselves that they would be better off going back to Egypt.

The sad part is that they weren't really defeated at all. God was meeting their every need. He gave them food and water. He led them through the wilderness. He fought their battles, provided for them, and protected them. Nothing had truly defeated them. The problem is that they surrendered. They quit trying. In essence, they defeated themselves.

Now, I know that many people are under the impression that the Christian life is a bed of roses. To them I say, "Roses have thorns!" The Christian walk is not a life of ease. It is full of troubles and trials, and yes, there will be battles that we can't win. But, no matter the outcome, we cannot allow defeat to keep us from going forward. I'm reminded of a line from a movie, "Never give up. Never surrender." That ought to be the Christian battle cry.

What would have happened if Christ had given up that day on the cross? Salvation wouldn't be an option. Heaven would be forever out of reach. I'm sure He was tired, discouraged, and feeling defeated. He was bruised and bleeding. His friends had all forsaken Him. Even His own Father couldn't bear to look at Him. Weary and in pain, He hung there alone, bearing upon Himself the weight of wrongs that He had not done.

Yet, He pressed on, and because of that, with His dying breath He shouted, "It is finished," which can be translated to "I have won!" What others interpreted as defeat, He interpreted as victory. He ran the race and finished His course. He urges us to do the same. Don't let defeat discourage you from your ministry in life, for one day it might become a great victory. One thing is for sure – you'll never know unless you keep on keeping on!

Dart # 7 – Discontentment

Did you know that there are twice as many shopping malls in America as there are high schools? Why? Because we are a people who are never satisfied with what we have and are always seeking to obtain more. We've all seen the bumper stickers. "More is better." "He who dies with the most toys wins." "Who says money can't buy happiness?" More, more, more. It's all about wanting more.

I wonder how many people are over their heads in debt simply because they weren't satisfied with what they had. Now, don't get me wrong. I personally know some people who are in a lot of debt because of physical illness, job loss, and things of that nature. These are not the people I'm talking about. I'm talking about the ones who have to have the latest and greatest. And, I'll admit, I've been down that road. Some purchases were legitimate needs. Others were things that I felt I should have either because someone else had it or because I told myself that I could be more and do more if I had it. Discontentment can lead us down a VERY long road!

Look at the crimes in the world today, and you'll see a pattern. Adultery occurs when someone is not content with the marriage partner he/she has, so that person goes looking in "greener pastures." Theft happens when someone feels they are entitled to more than what they have. Murder is often the result of arguments that revolve around issues of discontentment. On and on the list goes. When we focus on what we don't have instead of what we do have, trouble is bound to show up.

Discontentment isn't always based on material things. Often times we are discontent about the circumstances in our lives. We have a plan for our lives, and we get very upset when things don't work out the way we think they should. When illness strikes or a job is lost, discontentment can set in. When our new job is not as great as we thought it would be, our heart begins longing for more. In this way, discontentment causes us to lose precious hours playing the "what if" and "if only" games. You know, the ones where we say, "What if I had a million dollars in the bank account?" or "If only I were in better health. . ." These thoughts, though entertaining, do nothing but drain us of time and energy and cause us to sink deeper in our discontentment. We must be on guard.

The Bible doesn't say much about discontentment, but it has a lot to say about contentment. Let's look at a few of these verses.

- *And the soldiers likewise demanded of him, saying, And what shall we do? And he said unto them, Do violence to no man, neither accuse any falsely; and be content with your wages. (Luke 3:14)*

- *Not that I speak in respect of want: for I have learned, in whatsoever state I am, therewith to be content. (Philippians 4:11)*

- *But godliness with contentment is great gain. (I Timothy 6:6)*

- *And having food and raiment let us be therewith content. (I Timothy 6:8)*

- *Let your conversation be without covetousness; and be content with such things as ye have: for he hath said, I will never leave thee, nor forsake thee. (Hebrews 13:5)*

While the Bible doesn't use the word "discontentment," it illustrates it on many of its pages. Sarai was not content to wait on God's promised son, so she hatched up a plan of her own. The children of Israel were not content with the provision that God supplied, so they turned from Him and began worshiping idols. Ahab was not content with all his lands and riches. He had to take Naboth's vineyard as well. David was not content with his own wife, so he took the wife of another man. Jacob was not content with God's promise, so he tricked his father into giving him the blessing. Over and over again, we see discontent worming its way into the lives of good people and bad.

If you'll study each of the above stories, you'll find that there are always consequences for discontentment. Often times, however, the consequences don't affect only the guilty party. It is imperative that we keep in mind that our discontentment can hurt other people as well. After all, some of the consequences of the above stories are still taking place today. One little mistake can have a lifetime of repercussions.

I think one of the main problems we have is that we don't fully understand the meaning of the word "content." When we think of contentment, we think of having everything we want and being happy and satisfied. But, that's not the true meaning of contentment. There is so much more involved in being content. It's not simply having everything we want. It's being able to rest in the knowledge that we have everything we need. It's being able to look at life and say, "Well, it's not what I had planned, but it's what God allowed, and I know He knows what's best for me." Contentment takes our eyes off ourselves and our circumstances and places them where they belong – on God.

For that reason, the best cure for discontentment is thankfulness. As long as we're dwelling on what we don't have, discontentment will hang around. But, as soon as we start noticing all the ways that we've been blessed, things will start to turn around. I like the old song, "Count Your Blessings." It reminds us that we cannot fathom how much God has done for us, and as hard as we may try, we'll never be able to name all the blessings He's given us. We are a blessed people. Why do we forget that? Why doesn't that satisfy us?

It will if we keep our eyes and thoughts focused. Who cares what kind of car the neighbors have? Who cares if one of our best friends has "the perfect life"? Who cares if things are not turning out the way we planned? Who's better at planning anyway – us or God?

With all that being said, there is one good side to discontentment. In the proper areas of our lives, discontentment can inspire us to improve. For example, I am not content with my Christian walk. I feel that I need to be closer to the Lord. I am not satisfied with the amount of time I spend with Him. I am not happy with the sins that I commit over and over again. Because of this discontentment, I try harder. The dissatisfaction with my Christian walk urges me to do better each and every day. In this way, discontentment can be a good thing.

God does not want us to be without ambitions or goals. He wants us to strive harder, to grow, to become more like Him. What He doesn't want is for us to constantly grumble and complain about all the things that we want but don't have. It's almost like waving our fists in God's face and saying, "You messed up. You didn't do it right. I wanted things to go this way, and they didn't. It's your fault. Fix it."

Sounds like a spoiled brat, doesn't it? Unfortunately, that's sometimes how we act — like spoiled children who aren't getting our way. We pout. We cry. We try to figure out ways to "fix the problem."

If only we would sit back and realize that the problem lies not in what we don't have but in how ungrateful we are for what we do have. We need to take the advice of I Thessalonians 5:18, *In every thing give thanks.* Notice, it doesn't say "**For** every thing give thanks." It says, "**In** every thing give thanks." It would be silly to say that I should be thankful that my husband lost his job. However, because my husband lost his job, we've been able to spend a lot of time together. Therefore, in the midst of this trying time, I can be thankful.

I urge you to try it today. Look at the situations around you that may have you feeling discontent and ask yourself,

"How can I be thankful in this situation?" You may be surprised at the answers you find.

****

A man in the desert was craving something to drink and saw a lemonade stand on the next sand dune. He ran to it, but when he arrived, the lemonade stand disappeared and reappeared on the next sand dune. When he ran to the next sand dune and grabbed for the lemonade, it disappeared and reappeared again on the next dune. He continued to chase it from dune to dune until he died of thirst. He was only chasing a mirage. Discontentment is a mirage that leads us on an endless chase and never satisfies our thirst. (Kent Crockett, "The 911 Handbook," Peabody, MA: Hendrickson Publishers, 2003)

Dart #8 – Distraction

This book was started months ago, and it doesn't really take very long to write a book of this size. So, what was the hold up? Distraction! It seemed like every time I began working on it, something else came up that was more important. Friends or family called with an urgent need, and I rushed to the rescue. The computer decided to take a vacation and left no forwarding address. The washing machine died. The vacuum cleaner blew up. Illness struck. I assure you, it was one thing after another. Sometimes, the interruptions were beyond my control, but often they were not.

Distraction is a thief. It will rob you of time, effort, and a sense of responsibility. Sadly, the world we live in today is FULL of distractions. Television. Internet. Cell phones. E-mail. Hobbies. Each of these things, in and of itself, is not bad. The problem occurs when we become so engrossed in these things that we completely lose track of time and obligations. And, if you haven't noticed, it's INCREDIBLY easy to get distracted.

Each morning, one of the first things I do is check my e-mail. Sometimes I can do it in less than five minutes. Sometimes it takes me much longer. Why? Because something catches my attention, and I just have to check it out. The Internet is the same way. I'll go online to research something, and end up spending 10 or 15 minutes looking at some funny cartoons I come across in the process. Then, I have to get my mind focused again on what I was doing, find my place, reorder my thoughts, etc. That takes another 10 or 15 minutes. Boom! I just wasted half an hour because I was distracted.

Computers, televisions, and cell phones are fine in moderation. But, God has placed us on this Earth, and He has given us each a job to do. How can we do our jobs if we're always sidetracked by something else? How can we honor Him if we're wasting the precious time He has given us?

A while back, we had a problem with yellow jackets in our yard. We had a square piece of plywood on the ground on which the barbecue grill sat. Somehow, the yellow jackets had worked their way under this plywood and built a huge nest.

We had noticed an abundance of the pesky creatures, but we couldn't figure out where they were coming from. However, they made a dreadful mistake – one of them stung my dog. The war was on! Nobody messes with my dogs!!!!

We finally discovered their hiding place and developed a plan. We waited until nightfall to ensure that all the yellow jackets were safely tucked away in their nest. Then Jason carefully tipped the plywood over, exposing the red earth beneath it. Sure enough, there was a large hole in the ground. He carefully poured kerosene into the hole and then set it on fire. Needless to say, the yellow jackets weren't happy. But, we were. . . until the next morning.

When I stepped out the back door the next morning, I was immediately bombarded by a swarm of angry yellow jackets. *How is that possible?* I thought. *How could we have missed so many?* It didn't take me long to find my answer.

As I looked around, I noticed that the yellow jackets weren't swarming around the blackened hole that had once been their nest (or so I thought.) No, they were hovering over the plywood. I looked closer. Sure enough, there was a HUGE nest attached to what had been the underside of the plywood. Jason had seen the hole and been so focused on it that he had failed to see the nest on the plywood. In his defense, it was dark during his first attack. His second assault was far more successful.

Do you see how distraction works? It jumps up and down waving its arms saying, "Look over here. See this? Here! Here! Look over here." And so, we look, taking our focus off the things that we really need to be doing. Sometimes, we do it knowingly. Other times, we don't even realize what we've done until much time has passed and we've gotten nothing accomplished.

The worst distraction of all for me is not the computer or the cell phone. It's not my husband or my dogs. It's not even the good book sitting on the shelf screaming, "Read me! Read me!" No, my worst source of distraction is my own mind. I literally drive myself crazy. My mind will not be still. It is constantly running in a million different directions at a speed that would rival an Air Force jet.

As I sit down each morning to do my devotions, my mind begins to wander. *What am I going to have for breakfast? I need to do some laundry today. Oh, did I ever pay the power bill? What should I write about in my blog? What was I reading?* And on and on it goes. I'll get my mind back on my reading, but within a couple of minutes, it's off in La La Land again.

I wish the problem stopped there, but it doesn't. As I sit in church, attempting to listen to the preaching, something is said that sets my mind off on another rabbit trail. The worst is song titles and lyrics. I love music, and I know a lot of songs. So, when someone quotes something from a song (and our preacher does this A LOT), my mind starts singing the song. Just about the time I get it reigned in, the preacher does it again. I literally have to fight myself and make myself listen. It's not that I don't want to hear the preaching of the Word of God, it's simply that I'm easily distracted.

Even as I lie in bed at night, my mind distracts me from my duty, which at that point is sleep. I toss and turn as I relive the events of the day and think about the things that need to be done tomorrow. My body is tired and begging for rest, but my mind is too distracted to notice.

You hear a lot lately about ADD. In fact, I know a lot of people who have been diagnosed as having ADD. What is ADD? Attention Deficit Disorder. In other words, easily distracted. Why is everyone treating this like it's something new? People have been distracted for centuries. This is not a new thing. I think it's just the world's way of excusing it and profiting from it. After all, you can't sell drugs to overcome distraction. People just wouldn't fall for it. So, let's give it a clinical name, diagnose people with it, and make some money.

I'm not denying that some people truly suffer from certain disorders and are in need of medication. But, I've seen children on ADD medications who no longer resemble children. They're more like zombies. I'm not a doctor, but to me, there was nothing wrong with the child. He/she was just a healthy, vivacious child who found it difficult to be still and focus. Aren't we all guilty of that from time to time? Does that mean we should all be on drugs?

Distraction is not a disease. It is a tool of the devil to pull our focus away from serving God. Distraction has us running rabbits and chasing dreams instead of fulfilling the ministry we've been called to be a part of. It comes in many forms, but the result is always the same – unfinished work.

Hebrews 12:1-2 says, *Wherefore seeing we also are compassed about with so great a cloud of witnesses, let us lay aside every weight, and the sin which doth so easily beset us, and let us run with patience the race that is set before us, Looking unto Jesus the author and finisher of our faith; who for the joy that was set before him endured the cross, despising the shame, and is set down at the right hand of the throne of God.*

First of all, let's look at the phrase, *let us lay aside every weight, and the sin which doth so easily beset us.* That sounds like distraction to me. What do you think? We are in a race, and that race becomes very difficult to run when we're dragging around extra weight and not paying attention to where we're going. Think back to any races you've ever seen. Are the runners looking around at the crowds? No. Are they looking at the other racers? No. Are they looking at the path that they've already covered? No. Where are they looking? At the finish line. Their eyes are focused on their goal. If their concentration wavers for even an instant, they may lose precious seconds, causing them to lose the race. Likewise, we must keep our focus on the finish line. Jesus did.

Look at the beginning of verse two. *Looking unto Jesus. . .who for the joy that was set before him endured the cross.* As Jesus hung in agony of the cross, I believe He was clearly focused on His goal. Yes, I'm sure He saw the chaos that was going on around Him, but that didn't distract Him. I believe, as He hung on that cross, He was looking into Heaven and seeing the mansions that would one day house His children. I believe He was envisioning an eternity filled with the saints of the ages gathered around the throne and singing praises.

The verse talks about the joy that was set before Him. What joy? Heaven? He could have had that without dying. In fact, He left Heaven to come and die for our sins. Why? What joy could He possibly be looking forward to? The only answer I can come up with is spending eternity with us, and if that doesn't thrill your soul, I don't know what will. Jesus was looking forward to our salvation, our acceptance of His work. He didn't allow His pain and agony to distract Him from doing what He needed to do so that we could live forever with Him. He did what he promised in John 4:34, *Jesus saith unto them, My meat is to do the will of him that sent me, and to* ***finish his work.***

Jesus finished His work. Have we finished ours, or are we constantly fighting distraction? Just as with the other darts, the best way to fight off distraction is to immerse ourselves in God's Word and to keep our focus on Him. We must ask Him for strength to help us accomplish what needs to be done without distraction. He knows how difficult it is for us, and He will help us. After all, it's His work we are trying to finish.

Dart #9 – Deceit

I honestly believe that deceit dates back to the time when Lucifer deceived himself into thinking he could be God. He was a great angel, a beautiful creature. He had the honor of being close to the King of Kings. He had the privilege of worshiping the Lord of Lords. But, that was not enough for him. His discontentment led him to fool himself into thinking that he was just as good and as powerful as God Himself. With those thoughts, he led a rebellion, resulting in being cast from Heaven along with his companions, a third of all the angels. Could it have been that they were deceived, too? Probably.

Satan is know as the "father of lies," and for good reason. The next time he appears on the scene, he is deceiving Eve. *Ye shall not surely die: for God doth know that in the day ye eat thereof, then your eyes shall be opened, and ye shall be as gods, knowing good and evil.* Here, Satan's deceit, along with man's disobedience, led to the fall of mankind, and the pattern continues.

Satan's goal in life is to keep us from trusting in the saving blood of Christ. For many, he fulfills that goal by convincing them that they don't need God. He reminds them of all that they've been able to accomplish on their own. He assures them that God does not have their best interests at heart. He offers them the lies of evolution in order to deny the existence and power of the Lord. Just as with Eve, he speaks to them of freedom from rule and the ability to be their own gods. Though his declarations are false, he appeals to many, causing them to deny Christ and live for their own pleasure.

When Satan fails at his ultimate goal, as he did when each of us was saved, he uses his deceitfulness in a new way. Rather than convincing us that we don't need God, he uses other lies to weaken our faith. Here are some of the most common lies that he uses:

- God doesn't love you.

- You aren't worthy of God's love.

- If you do wrong, no one will ever find out.

- Everyone has to break the rules sometimes.

- God is too busy to be burdened with your petty problems.

- You'll never amount to anything.

- God has let you down.

- God has forsaken you, and now you're all alone.

- God can't keep all of His promises.

- That sin is unforgivable.

Sadly, the list goes on and on. Satan is not dumb like many people think. Satan is crafty. He knows which lie to hit us with and when to hit us with it. He knows when we are the most vulnerable and therefore, the most likely to fall for his deceitfulness. He doesn't come to us when we're on the mountain top, praising God and full of peace. No, he waits until we're in the valley. He waits until the tears fall. Then, he comes to us in his insidious way. Dumb? No. Sneaky? Absolutely.

The dart of deceit works in two ways. One is when Satan deceives us. The second way is when deceive each other. Whether it be in outright lies, "little white lies," exaggerations, or omissions of the truth, deceitfulness has caused many problems throughout history.

When most of us think of deceit, we think of flat out lies. You know, the simple black and white truth. ***Did you take a cookie? No.*** If we really did take the cookie, we lied. We deceived someone. That concept is pretty simple for us to grasp. It's the other types of deceit that we seem to have trouble with.

Let me take this opportunity to say that there is no such thing as a "little white lie." I don't know where that phrase came from, but a lie is a lie. It doesn't matter how big it is, a lie is a lie. Case closed.

But, what about exaggerations? Are those considered lies? They should be because they do deceive people. We are all familiar with the term "fish stories." It's usually said with a laugh because we all picture some fisherman catching a fish about the size of a young girl's sandal, but by the time he's finished telling his tale, the fish is at least the size of a large boot. He exaggerated. He deceived people into thinking that the fish was larger than it actually was.

Don't we often do the same? Maybe not with fish, but with other things. We tell people we stood in line for hours, when in actuality, we were only there for 15 minutes. Perhaps we exaggerate our abilities. Sometimes we exaggerate our circumstances. And, for want of a good story, sometimes we exaggerate events in our lives. While it may seem harmless, it's still wrong. It's still deceit. We need to be careful.

Then, there is the omission of truth. This is when we don't come right out and tell a lie, but neither do we tell the truth that would clear up a matter. For an example of that, I'm going to tell you a story that I've told to very few people because I am still so ashamed of it.

When I was in third grade, my teacher gave the class a penmanship assignment. We were to pick a poem out of our reading book and copy it. The assignment was going to be counted as a test grade, so we were told to do our very best. I wasn't overly concerned, for penmanship was one of my best subjects. I've always had very neat handwriting (although I don't always use it). I completed the assignment and took it home to show my parents.

When I showed it to my mom, she looked at it for a few minutes and then asked me, "Did you write this." Beaming with pride, I smiled and nodded my head. She ran to show it to my dad who seemed a little surprised by my work but praised me nonetheless. "I didn't know you could write poetry," he said.

Suddenly, it hit me. When my mom asked if I had written the poem, she wasn't referring to my penmanship. She was referring to the authorship. They were both now under the impression that I had authored the poem. I didn't mean to lie. I simply misunderstood her question. So, I had a choice to make. Sadly, instead of speaking up and admitting to the mistake, I let them continue to believe that I had indeed written the poem.

I had a guilty conscience anyway, but things grew worse when my mom insisted on showing the poem to everyone she met. She was so proud of me, and the prouder she became, the harder it was for me to tell her the truth. She was so happy, and I knew it would break her heart if I told her that I had deceived her. Still, with each time she boasted of my work, I cringed. The guilt was killing me. I had to tell her the truth.

I will never forget the look of disappointment in my mother's eyes. At first, she could not even speak to me. She only looked at me with tear-filled eyes and then shook her head. I knew she was hurt. I knew she was disappointed. Worst of all, I knew that if I had simply explained the misunderstanding at the beginning, it would have saved both of us a great deal of heartache. Whether the lie is plain spoken or an omission of the truth, it still hurts people and causes a lot of trouble. This is a lesson I will never forget.

Dart #10 – Disagreements

Whenever I think of disagreements in the Bible, the story of Cain and Abel comes immediately to mind. We know that God commanded sacrifices to be done in a certain way. Abel obeyed that way. Cain didn't, and when God refused his sacrifice, he became angry and slew his own brother. I'm not sure if Cain was in a disagreement with Abel or with God. I tend to think he disagreed with God, but took his anger out on his brother. Just my opinion. Whatever the case, there was a disagreement, and in the end, there was a murder.

Just as with many of the other darts, disagreement itself is not a sin. We are all different people and therefore, we see things differently. We have different likes and dislikes. We have different personalities. We have different opinions on many different topics. Disagreements are bound to happen. It is how we handle those disagreements that makes the difference. For example, take a look at some of the news headlines I came across while researching this chapter:

- *"Professor leaving school after disagreement"*
- *"Disagreement between business partners leads to murder-suicide at pawn shop"*
- *"Friends' disagreement leads to murder"*
- *"Domestic disagreement leads to high-speed chase"*

These were just a few that I came across in a matter of minutes. The newspaper is full of stories of murder, theft, etc. that all started because of disagreements. Evidently, these people did not know or did not care to handle the disagreement in the right way. Instead, they let it fester to the point that an aggressive action seemed to be the only resolution.

Satan loves to sow discord. And, to be honest, sometimes it's not a very hard job. What do I mean? Simply that one of the main causes of disagreements is pride. We all have it. Some of us have more than others, but all of us have enough to lead to an argument every now and then. We don't like to be wrong, but even more than that, we don't like to be told that we're wrong. That's basically what a disagreement is. It's two people (sometimes more) trying to get the other one to see his/her point of view.

That, in itself, is not a problem. But, we are so proud and so stubborn sometimes that we convince ourselves that our point of view is the only one that matters, and we refuse to even try to see what the other person is saying. This leads to frustration for the other person, not to mention a blow to his/her pride. And, then, you have an argument — each person trying to convince the other that he is right. This, in turn, leads to hard feelings, anger, resentment, etc.

If only we could learn to deal with our pride, I believe there would be a lot fewer disagreements. Instead, one person would sit down and express his/her opinion while the other listened and tried to understand. Then, roles would reverse. In the end, each person would understand the other person better and would be able to look at the topic from both sides.

That doesn't mean that they would necessarily agree on the topic, but sometimes we have to agree to disagree. When each person has made his/her point and each person understands where the other person is coming from, there is nothing else to be done. Either the two agree or they don't. Arguing about it won't change either of their minds. Sure, one may give in for the sake of peace, but deep down, his feelings about the issue haven't changed. The solution? Acknowledge that you are each entitled to your opinion and go on with life. Why waste the time arguing about things that really don't matter in the long run?

The best way to handle disagreements is by having good communication skills. Many people equate communication with talking, but communication is a two-way street. It involves talking and listening. In order to solve a disagreement, both talking and listening must be present.

The problem most of us run into is that we are so heated in the disagreement that we talk plenty but don't really listen to what the other person is saying. Yes, we may be hearing, but hearing and listening are not the same thing. Listening involves taking in the things that we are hearing and processing them so that we can understand them better. Instead, we are often too busy thinking of what we're going to say when it's our turn to talk instead of listening to the other person. It's no wonder the disagreements don't get solved and instead lead to catastrophes.

Disagreements are the cause of many divorces, broken friendships, and split churches. Disagreements have touched every household in one way or another. We must learn to deal with them in the proper way. We must get rid of our pride and work on our communication skills. This would solve a lot of problems, not to mention help us to grow spiritually.

It won't be easy, but it is possible. God will help. His Word is full of advice on how to extinguish our pride. The Bible is the ultimate guide on how to communicate with one another. If we will spend time in it and apply the things we learn, we're bound to see improvement in our lives. Plus, we'll be able to fight off a few more deadly darts.

Conclusion

Please be aware that the devil's arsenal is much greater than just the ten things I've mentioned in this book. He is a dangerous enemy, and he will stop at nothing to ruin our lives. His power is great and his weapons are many. Alone, we do not stand a chance.

Isn't it good to know that we are not alone? Isn't it a blessed thought to know that even though the devil is powerful, God is more powerful? Yes, we should be wary of the devil and his darts, but we do not need to fear him. He is no match for our God.

I hope that throughout this book, you've read some thoughts that have helped you. I know that there is nothing new in this book. In fact, all good things in this book came from THE BOOK. However, I also know that sometimes we need to be reminded of things. Sometimes, we need to look at things from a different point of view. Sadly, sometimes we're more prone to read a book than we are to read God's Word.

My purpose is writing this book is not to draw you away from the Bible. If anything, it is to draw you to it. It, alone, contains the answers you seek and the knowledge you need to fight off the attacks of the devil. We've all heard the saying, "You can lead a horse to water, but you can't make him drink." Similarly, I can lead you to the answers, but it's up to you to follow. I pray that God will help you in your journey.

* *

For daily encouragement, go to
www.DanaRongione.blogspot.com and
www.ChristianSongoftheDay.blogspot.com.

God bless you!

Printed in Great Britain
by Amazon

19417489R00051